Mommadele's
Easy Dinner Ideas for College Students
31 Shortcut Recipes for Hungry Students
on a Budget and a Time Crunch

By Adele M. Gill

Dedication

Mommadele's Easy Dinner Ideas for College Students: 31 Shortcut Recipes for Hungry Students on a Budget and a Time Crunch is dedicated to my wonderful husband, Phil, and our 2 grown children, Jessie and Tim.

May this cooking guide provide quick, easy, nutritious, and cost-saving meals for generations of new cooks living independently on their own.

Preface

Congratulations on your newly found independence, and welcome to *Mommadele's Easy Dinner Ideas for College Students!*

This cooking guide *is* chock-full of simple recipes, one for every day of the month. In fact, this shortcut cooking guide offers delicious dinners using a microwave, stove, oven and/or CrockPot. These meals are designed to share with roommates and friends or use as time-saving leftovers for later in the week.

College students today are most often well-prepared for every aspect of college life. However, if you are like my own 2 grown children, a crash course in cooking may be helpful, as cooking is a new experience for many college students, hence the reason for this cookbook! Sure, everyone knows how to make ramen noodles, and egg and cheese sandwiches. But there is so much more to eating a well-balanced diet on a shoestring budget!

This cookbook provides simple recipes that save money, time and energy, are inexpensive, 'Almost-like-Mom's' recipes, many using just 5 or less ingredients. Most recipes involve using just one pan, for quick and easy clean-up, and they provide ample food to share with friends or use as leftovers for later in the week. These time-tested favorites may be decreased in half to feed 1 with leftovers, or doubled to feed a crowd.

From Tijuana Tacos to Hearty Pot Roast to Asian Rice Bowls to Chicken Cacciatore, this cookbook has a variety of ethnic and traditional American dishes, recipes sure to appeal to your taste buds and plenty for leftovers or to share. Recipes can be doubled to make for a crowd, or halved to make smaller portions.

Special care has been given to create diverse recipes that are pleasing to the senses of taste, sight and smell, and especially to remind you of your own Mom's cooking.

Whether cooking for yourself or for a crowd, this cooking guide was written especially for Y-O-U. I hope you will enjoy and benefit from *Mommadele's Easy Dinner Ideas for College Students* and will share this book and these recipes with your family and friends for years to come!

Best,
Mommadele

Table of Contents

#1 Tijuana Tacos
Stove Setting: Medium   Cooking Time: 20 minutes

Serves 4

Ingredients:
8 Soft flour or hard corn taco shells
1 pound Ground beef
1 packet Taco seasoning
2 cups Cheddar Cheese
2 cups Shredded lettuce
Chunky Salsa [Optional]

Taco Directions:
Brown ground beef in frying pan until brown. Add taco seasoning packet with 1/3-1/2 cup water. Stir.

While meat is cooking, warm stack of soft tacos and hard corn tacos in microwave for 40 seconds with wet paper towel on top.

Place tortillas or taco shells, taco meat, lettuce, diced tomatoes, salsa and shredded cheese on table to serve.

Tacos for a Crowd:
To make tacos for a crowd, increase beef to 2 pounds, use 2 packets of taco seasoning, and 16 soft flour or hard corn taco shells.

CROCKPOT RECIPE
#2 Chicken Cacciatore
Cooking Time: 6-8 hours   CrockPot Setting: Low
Serves 4

Ingredients:
4 chicken breasts, uncooked
1 large container of prepared Spaghetti Sauce.
[Prego or Ragu are really good]
½ Onion
½ green pepper
2 cups water
1 pound dry spaghetti, penne or spiral pasta
Parmesan-Romano cheese [Optional]

Directions:
Rinse chicken in water and place in Crock Pot.

Add all other ingredients, except the spaghetti, into the CrockPot and turn it on the low setting.

You will come home to a great smelling house and dinner will be practically ready when you arrive…

All you need to do is cook the pasta for 9-12 minutes the way you like it, and serve with a salad and/or Italian bread!

Chicken Cacciatore Variation:
May be served in sauce or on the side.

To feed a crowd, double all ingredients, including pasta. Cook in large 6 or 7 quart slow cooker.

#3 Asian Rice Bowls
Cooking Time: 12 minutes　　　Stove Settings: Medium　　Serves 4

Ingredients:
4 cups cooked chicken, beef or pork
1 bundle fresh broccoli
Shaved carrots
1 jar Asian Panda Orange Sauce
½ cup canned, salted peanuts
2 packages Uncle Ben's Ready Rice

Directions:
Mix meat, broccoli, carrots and Asian Panda Orange Sauce in Wok or large frying pan. Stir mixture and sauté until hot and tender.

While that is cooking, prepare Uncle Ben's Microwaveable Ready Rice (takes just 90 seconds per bag in microwave).

Place rice in bowls or on plates, and top with meat and veggie mixture. Top with peanuts.

Variation: To decrease servings, halve recipe. To feed a crowd, simply double ingredients. For extra heat, drizzle with Siracha Sauce to make it spicy.

CROCKPOT RECIPE
#4 Hearty Pot Roast
Cooking Time: 6-8 hours   CrockPot Setting: Low Serves 4

Ingredients:
2 ½ -3 pound beef chuck roast
2 cans Whole New Potatoes
½ bag baby carrots or Baby Carrot Chips
1 Onion
1 Onion soup packet
2 cups water

Hearty Pot Roast Directions:

Open and drain potatoes. Cut beef into 4 large, even pieces and place in CrockPot with veggies and water. Cover and cook on low for 6-8 hours. The meat and veggies will be very tender, but not over cooked. This meal is perfect for busy days when you come home too tired to cook!

Variations:

Double all ingredients and cook in large 6 or 7 quart slow cooker. Serves 8. To thicken pot roast broth, add 2 tablespoons of Wondra Flour Mix (thickener) and stir. Let set for 5 minutes before stirring again and serving.

#5 Tim's Tex Mex
Cooking time: 15 minutes   Stovetop setting: Medium
Serves 4

Ingredients:
1 large can of canned chicken
(from the tuna aisle at the grocery store)
Or
1 cup leftover baked chicken with skin removed
2 large cans of corn
1 can black beans
1 packet Taco Seasoning
1 can spicy Rotel tomatoes
1 package Uncle Ben's Microwave Ready Rice, any flavor

Directions.
Open all cans and empty contents into a large 12 inch skillet. Mix all ingredients together in the skillet, including bag of Ready Rice.

Do not put rice in microwave.
Heat mixture in skillet until steamy hot and chicken is done. Serve on dinner size plate, or in a large bowl.

Tim's Tex Mex Variations:
To decrease servings, halve recipe. To feed a crowd, simply double ingredients. To increase servings, double recipe.

#6 Busy Day Baked Chicken
Easiest meal ever!

Baking time: 40 minutes   Oven setting: 425^0

Serves 4

Ingredients:
8 pieces of chicken
Season All Season Salt

Busy Day Baked Chicken Directions:
Rinse chicken and place in 13 x 9 inch rectangular pan. Preheat oven to 425^0.

Place chicken in pan in oven, uncovered for 40 minutes.
Voila!

Serving Suggestion:
Great with baked potato, baked sweet potato, Uncle Ben's Microwave Ready Rice or Creamy Mac & Cheddar Cheese.

Variations:
To decrease servings, halve recipe. To feed a crowd, simply double ingredients.

May drizzle with Buffalo Sauce for a special treat.

STOVETOP RECIPE
#7 Creamy Mac & Cheddar Cheese
Baking time: 20 minutes   Oven setting: 425°

Serves 4

Ingredients:
1 box elbow macaroni
2 cups mild shredded cheddar cheese
1 cup milk
Olive oil
½ sleeve Ritz Crackers for topping
Salt & Pepper

Creamy Mac and Cheddar Cheese Directions:
Empty macaroni box into a 5 quart pot of boiling water. Stir and cook pasta as directed on box.

When done, pour into strainer and then place pasta in 13 x 9 rectangular pan, add milk, and stir. Drizzle with olive oil, add cheddar cheese and salt and pepper to taste. Top with hand-crumbled Ritz Crackers. Bake uncovered in pan in 425 degree oven for 20-30 minutes. Enjoy!

Variations:
To decrease servings, halve recipe.

To feed a crowd, simply double ingredients and use a second rectangular pan.

Doubled recipe serves 8 people.

#8 Enrique Enchiladas
Baking time: 20 minutes   Oven setting: 425^0

Serves 4

Ingredients:

4 flat, 8 inch flour tortillas, any brand
1 large can Old El Paso Enchilada sauce
3 cups cooked chicken or canned chicken
3 cups shredded mild cheddar cheese

Chunky Salsa [optional]

Directions:
Spray bottom of 13 x 9 inch rectangular pan with Pam Vegetable Oil.

Place 2/3 cup of cut up or diced chicken in middle of flat flour tortilla.
Sprinkle chicken with mild cheddar cheese.

Roll snugly with ends open, and place in rectangular pan.
Top enchiladas with Old El Paso Enchilada Sauce and bake at 425
degrees for 20 minutes.

Variation:
May use shredded beef and/or top with shredded lettuce, onions, sliced
olives or jalapenos.

STOVETOP RECIPE
#9 Greek Omelet
Great for breakfast, lunch or dinner...Anytime!
Cooking Time: 15 minutes   Stove setting: Medium   Serves 4

Greek Omelet Ingredients:
6 eggs
1 handful fresh spinach
¼ cup feta cheese
PAM Cooking Spray
Salt & pepper

Directions:
Spray small skillet with PAM Cooking Spray. Break eggs in bowl and whip with fork to break the yolks. Pour eggs in heated pan and salt and pepper to taste. Toss spinach and feta cheese onto eggs and cook on medium heat and cook until eggs are no longer runny.

Fold omelet in half in pan, serve hot.

Variations:
May replace feta with ½ cup of Cheddar cheese or Swiss cheese inside and on top.

Also, may add cooked bacon, diced ham or sausage, chopped, sautéed onions, green or red peppers, fresh tomatoes.

CrockPot Recipe
#10 Cranberry Pork Chops
Cooking Time: 6-8 hours   CrockPot Setting: Low
Serves 4

Cranberry Pork Chops Ingredients:
4 pork chops
½ can jellied cranberry sauce
½ can whole cranberry sauce
½ bottle French dressing
1 ½ cups water

Directions
Place pork chops in a CrockPot. Mix all other ingredients with a fork, stir in 1 ½ cups water and pour over pork chops. Cook in CrockPot for 6-8 hours. Enjoy!

Variation:
May replace whole cranberry sauce with jellied cranberry sauce for a smoother texture.

To decrease servings, halve recipe. To feed a crowd, simply double ingredients.

May also bake in a 13 x 9 pan in the oven on 425 degrees for 25 minutes instead of using CrockPot.

Great with Uncle Ben's Microwaveable Ready Rice, Pennsylvania Dutch Egg Noodles, or instant mashed potatoes.

CROCKPOT RECIPE

#11 Saucy Mushroom Chicken

Cooking Time: 6-8 hours   CrockPot Setting: Low
Serves 4

Ingredients:
8 pieces of bone-in or boneless chicken
2 regular cans of Campbell's Cream of Mushroom Soup
Salt & pepper
1 ½ cups water

Directions:
Rinse chicken in water and place in CrockPot. Salt & pepper the
uncooked chicken.

Mix Campbell's cream of Mushroom Soup with 1 ½ cups water per
can and pour over chicken.

Cook in CrockPot for 6-8 hours. Yum!

Variation:
To feed a crowd, simply double ingredients.

May add 1 cup fresh mushrooms, chopped onions if you have them.

Serve with Uncle Ben's Microwave Ready Rice, Pennsylvania Dutch
Egg Noodles, or instant mashed potatoes.

Top with grated parmesan for extra flavor.

#12 Fiesta Fajitas

Cooking Time: 20 minutes   Stove Setting: Medium

Serves 4

Fiesta Fajita Ingredients:

2 cups cooked or canned chicken or shredded beef pieces
2 red & green peppers
1 medium onion
2 cups frozen broccoli
1 fajita seasoning packet
8 medium tortillas
2 tablespoon olive oil

Directions:

Chop onions and peppers into strips and place in medium heated skillet or Wok with 2 tbsp. of olive oil.

Sauté until tender, but do not overcook.

Serve fajitas right from pan.

Warm soft tortillas in microwave oven with a wet paper towel on top for 2 minutes.

Variations:

To decrease servings, halve recipe.

To feed a crowd, simply double ingredients to serve 8.

For extra color and flavor, may use yellow and/or green zucchini.

#13 Almost Home-Style Spaghetti

Cooking time: 6-8 hours   CrockPot setting: Low   Serves 4

Ingredients:
1 medium jar of chunky, spaghetti sauce with mushrooms
1 pound ground beef / 80-93 percent low-fat
1 medium green pepper
2 teaspoons minced garlic
1 box of spaghetti
2 tablespoons of olive oil
Grated Parmesan-Romano cheese (optional)

Almost Home-style Spaghetti Directions:
Spoon chopped garlic and olive oil into warm CrockPot.

Cut pepper in half and remove core and all seeds. Then cut pepper into strips and place in CrockPot with beef, and onion.

Pour sauce from jar over pepper, onion and beef, and cook together in CrockPot on Low heat.

Let cook for 6-8 hours on low heat.

When ready to eat, while the sauce is cooking, boil water for the pasta and cook pasta for approximately 9 minutes.

Test for doneness.

To serve:
Serve the spaghetti in a large bowl with the spaghetti sauce on top. Add parmesan cheese as desired.

Variations:
Double recipe and cook per above directions to serve 8 people.

May use thin spaghetti, angel hair, penne, spirals, or linguine pasta. May also substitute spaghetti squash for a low carb, low calorie option.

To cook spaghetti squash, cut in half length-wise and remove seeds from halves. Microwave for 12 minutes until stringy when flaked with a fork. Empty all of spaghetti squash strands into large bowl, drizzle with olive oil, and salt and pepper to taste.
Mangia!

For a special cost-saving, nutritious treat, or for every day, try this recipe with tuna or salmon!

TOASTER OVEN or OVEN RECIPE

#14 Best Easy Maryland Crab Cakes

Cooking time: 5 minutes   Oven Settings: Broil on low

Serves 4

Ingredients:

1 pound back fin crab meat or claw meat
(Claw meat is cheaper and sweeter)
1 packet of Old Bay Crab Cake Classic Mix
½ cup mayonnaise

Cocktail Sauce Ingredients:

¾ cup Heintz Ketchup
1 teaspoon grated horseradish

Crab Cake Directions:

Place Crab Cake Mix and mayonnaise in bowl. Gently add in crab meat, and gently fold the three ingredients together so crab does not flake apart.

Carefully measure 1/4 cup of crab meat mixture in measuring cup and place onto greased toaster oven pan with crab cakes 2 inches apart. Broil on top shelf of oven on low until light brown on top. Do not overcook. Serve with cocktail sauce or tartar sauce and cut lemon for garnish. To make, mix ketchup and horseradish together with a fork until fully blended. Serve on the side with your crab cakes.

Variations:

For cost-savings, may replace crab with canned salmon or albacore tuna. Simply flake tuna or salmon, add mix and mayonnaise and broil per directions above.

#15 Easy Thai Stir Fry
Cooking Time: 20 minutes   Stove Setting: Medium

Serves 4

Ingredients:
½ large bag of frozen Birds Eye Thai Stir Fry w/ soy sauce packet
[In freezer section]
2 cups cooked chicken, pork or beef cut
Microwaveable Uncle Ben's Ready Rice, uncooked
4 tablespoons virgin (pure) olive oil

Directions:
Heat Wok on medium heat and add olive oil to pan.

Place Frozen Thai Stir Fry veggies in large heated Wok or frying pan with sauce from pouch in bag, add meat and uncooked rice.

Sauté Thai Stir Fry vegetables, rice and meat until hot and tender. Add sauce packet from Thai Stir Fry package, heat and serve when steaming hot.

Variation:
May mix 2 tablespoon peanut butter with the soy sauce packet for extra Thai flavor.

CROCKPOT RECIPE
#16 Hawaiian BBQ Chicken
Cooking Time: 6-8 hours   CrockPot Setting: Low
Serves 4

Ingredients:
4 fresh boneless chicken breasts
1 can Pineapple chunks with juice
1 container BBQ sauce
1 ½ -2 cups water

Directions:
Rinse chicken breasts with water and place in CrockPot.

Top with BBQ sauce, pineapple with juice. Cook for 6-8 hours. Enjoy!

Variations:
To feed a crowd, chicken breasts may be replaced with 8 chicken breasts, cut in half (makes 8 pieces of chicken). Follow directions above, doubling pineapple and BBQ sauce. Serves 8.

CROCKPOT RECIPE
#17 Beef Chili for a Crowd
CrockPot Setting: Low   Cooking Time: 6-8 hours
Serves 8

Beef Chili For a Crowd Ingredients:
1 pound fresh or frozen ground beef, defrosted
3 large cans crushed tomatoes
1 small can tomato paste
1 green pepper
1 large onion
1 large can dark red kidney beans
1 cup water
1/4 cup Chili powder

Beef Chili Directions:
Mix all ingredients together in the CrockPot in the morning.

Turn CrockPot on Low and enjoy a complete slow-cooker meal in 6-8 hours!

Serve with French or Italian bread, corn bread or tortilla chips.

Variations:
Serve with shredded cheddar cheese or chopped onions.

CROCKPOT RECIPE
#18 White Chicken Chili
Cooking Time: 6-8 Hours   CrockPot Setting: Low
Serves 8

Ingredients:
3 cups canned chicken or fresh cubed chicken
½ sweet onion
3 cans whole potatoes
1 can Campbell's Cream of Mushroom Soup
1 can Campbell's Cream of Celery Soup
2 cups water

Directions:
Cut potatoes into 2 inch pieces and mix all ingredients together in the CrockPot in the morning.

Turn slow cooker on low for 6-8 hours to cook through the day, and enjoy a complete CrockPot dinner!

Serve with French, Italian bread, or corn bread.

Variations:
Double all ingredients and cook in large 6-7 quart slow cooker. Serve with shredded cheddar cheese. May add chopped onions or herbs, basil or cilantro.

CROCKPOT RECIPE
#19 Hot Italian Sausage,
Peppers & Onions
Cooking Time: 6-8 hours   Crock Pot Setting:
Serves 4

Ingredients:
1 package of 6 Hot Italian Sausages, uncooked
1 large onion
2 red or green peppers
2 cups water

Sausage, Pepper and Onion Directions:
Place hot sausages, together with onions and peppers in CrockPot.

Mix all ingredients together in the CrockPot in the morning.

Turn CrockPot on Low and 6-8 hours later, enjoy a delicious dinner!

Variations:
Try fat-free turkey sausage for low calorie alternative.

To serve 8 people, simply double recipe.

This recipe can also be done in the oven in a 13 x 9 baking dish, and baked for approximately 40 minutes on 400^0.

STOVETOP RECIPE
#20 Fried Rice
This high protein is easy and great for test days! Cooking Time: 20 minutes   Stove Setting: Medium
Serves 4

Fried Rice Ingredients:

2 cups cooked beef, chicken or pork, diced
1 ½ cup of SoyVay Soy Sauce
1 small bag, mixed vegetables
5 stalks green onion, chopped
1 egg
Microwaveable Uncle Ben's Ready Rice, unheated
3 tbsp. olive oil

Directions:
Place olive oil in Wok or large frying pan and heat until it sizzles.

Tear open rice package, add rice to Wok, and add rest of ingredients, except the egg. Toss mixture in pan.

When Fried Rice is hot all the way through, add egg with broken yolk (for extra protein) and stir rigorously with a wooden spoon to avoid scratching pan.

When egg is fully cooked, dish is ready to serve!

#21 Lo Mein
Cooking Time: 20-25 min.   Stove Settings: Medium Serves 4

Ingredients:
2 cups cooked meat: beef, chicken or pork
½ bottle SoyVay Soy Sauce
8-10 mini carrots
1 bundle broccoli, cut-up
4 stalks green onion or ¼ sweet onion, diced
½ - 2/3 box Linguine
3 tbsp. Olive oil

Lo Mein Directions:
Chop carrots in mini chopper. Place all ingredients (including chopped carrots and green onions) in heated Wok or large frying pan with 3 tbsp. olive oil.

Heat until soy sauce is bubbly hot, vegetables are heated, not overdone, then submerge dry linguine pasta into soy sauce base, in middle of Wok, and cook for 10-12 minutes longer. Dish is ready when pasta is al dente…just right! May serve with warmed egg rolls from freezer section at grocery store.

You and your friends will love this fun recipe…
Great for a party with friends or a special   mid-week
dinner!

OVEN RECIPE
#22 Boneless Buffalo Chicken
Cooking Time: 21 minutes   Oven Settings: 400^0
Serves 4

Buffalo Chicken Ingredients:
1 bag of Tyson or Perdue Breaded Chicken
Strips/boneless, frozen [Tyson or Perdue brands are good]
½ regular bottle of Franks Buffalo Wing Hot Sauce
4 stalks of celery, cut-up into 4 inch strips
1 cup Ranch dressing

Buffalo Chicken Directions:

Cook frozen breaded chicken strips in oven for about 18 minutes on 400^0.

Drizzle with Buffalo Wing Hot Sauce about 5 minutes before done and return to oven for about 5 minutes.

When ready to serve, garnish with celery and Ranch Dressing for dipping.

Serve with a salad. Enjoy!

Variations:

For Buffalo Chicken Salad, serve on top of a garden salad with ranch dressing drizzled on top, or with baked sweet potato fries from the freezer section of the grocery store. To decrease recipe, cut in half. To increase for a crowd, double all ingredients. Two bags of Breaded Chicken Strips serves 8 people.

STOVETOP RECIPE
#23 Swiss Veggie Burgers
Cooking Time: 12 minutes   Stove Setting: Medium
Serves 4

Ingredients:
4 Veggie Burgers
[Morningstar or Boca Burger brands]
4 Hamburger rolls
4 slices Swiss cheese
Lettuce
Tomato
Mayonnaise
Pam Cooking Spray

Swiss Veggie Burger Directions:

Spray bottom of frying pan with Pam Cooking Spray.

Place Veggie burgers in pan and cook on medium heat until desired doneness.

Remove from pan and place on burger.

Top burger with Swiss cheese, and melt cheese on burger in pan. Remove from pan.

Add mayonnaise, tomato and lettuce. Enjoy!

Variations:
Top with tomato, lettuce and mayo or sautéed onions, mushrooms, or cheddar cheese.

This healthy meal is high in antioxidants and Omega 3's!

OVEN RECIPE
#24 Baked Fish Pouches

Cooking Time: 30 minutes   Oven Settings: 400^0 Serves 4

Ingredients:
4 filets tilapia or salmon fish filets, frozen
4 small potatoes, skins on, sliced

3 stalks chopped green onions
1 teaspoon parsley
12 mini carrots
1 bundle fresh broccoli

Baked Fish Pouches Directions:
Place the fish on aluminum foil with potatoes, green onions, carrots and frozen broccoli.

Drizzle with olive oil and wrap tight in foil packets by wrapping the top edges, then folding the sides in (see above) so seal ingredients inside.

Place foil packets in preheated oven and bake at 400^0 for 30 minutes.

Variations:
May halve recipe to decrease servings, or double ingredients to make 8 servings. Any kind of frozen or fresh fish may be substituted for salmon or tilapia, including white fish or flounder. Also, any assortment of vegetables works with this meal including artichokes, hearts of palm, and zucchini.

OVEN RECIPE
#25 Chicken Pot Pie
Cooking Time: 35-40 minutes   Oven Settings: 425^0
Serves 4

Ingredients:
1 box of roll-out pie crust (contains 2 crusts)
2 cups chicken, cooked, diced or canned
1 small bag mixed vegetables
3 small potatoes, diced
1 can of Cream of Celery Soup
Pam Cooking Spray

Chicken Pot Pie Directions:
Take pie crusts out of package and let set on counter for 10-15 minutes
before using

Unroll 1 pie crust and place in 9 inch pie pan or deep baking dish lined
with Pam Cooking Spray.

Add chicken, bag of veggies, potatoes and Cream of Celery Soup into
pan.

Place second rolled pie crust on top.

Seal all around plate lip by pressing crust with a fork, and make 5 slits
on top of crust.

Place in 425^0 oven for about 35 minutes or until the crust is cooked
and light brown.

To Serve:
Great as a complete meal, with a salad and/or bread/rolls.

Variations:
For Beef Pot Pie, simply replace chicken with 2 cups of cubed beef cubed into 1 inch pieces. To expand recipe for a crowd of 8 people, double recipe and use a 13 x 9 rectangular pan. This version will only have a top crust. Cut top crust with pizza cutter forming dough strips and arrange and place on top.

Look how you mastered this one!

#26 Tuna Casserole
Baking Time: 30 minutes   Oven Settings: 425^0
Serves 4

Ingredients:
12-oz can Albacore Tuna packed in water, drained
1 can Campbell's Cream of Mushroom Soup
½ can green beans, drained
½ large bag Pennsylvania Dutch Egg Noodles
1 cup seasoned bread crumbs
1 cup water

Tuna Casserole Directions:
Boil 4 quarts of water in a tall pasta pan with a pinch of salt.
Place egg noodles in boiling water and cook as directed on package.
Drain tuna and green beans into sink.
While the water is boiling, spray pan bottom with PAM and place all
other ingredients, except bread crumbs, in a 13 x 9 rectangular pan or
3 quart size.

Stir in 1 cup water and preheat oven.

Top with breadcrumbs and bake in a 425^0 oven for 30 minutes.

Variations:
Double recipe serves 8 people.

May substitute 1 small bag of frozen green peas for the green beans.

#27 Kung Pao Chicken
Here's to an easy, spicy, fun dinner!
Cooking Time: 20 minutes   Oven Settings: 425^0 Serves 4

Ingredients:
4 cups cooked chicken (boneless), cut into 3 inch pieces
1 bundle Broccoli, frozen
2 tablespoon Siracha Sauce
½ jar Peanut butter
½ cup peanuts
2 tablespoons Olive oil

Kung Pao Chicken Directions:
Place chicken and broccoli in 13 x 9 rectangular pan

Mix Siracha and peanut butter together in a bowl, pour over chicken,
and broccoli florets.
Salt & pepper to taste.

Bake on low for 20 minutes. Top with peanuts after done baking in the
oven. Serve hot.

Double recipe and add an extra rectangular pan. Serves 8 people.

OVEN RECIPE
#28 Spicy Stuffed Shells
Bake for 40 minutes   Oven setting: 425^0

Serves 4

Ingredients:

½ large bag of froz. cheese stuffed shells (8 stuffed shells)

1 medium jar of chunky prepared spaghetti sauce

[Ragu or Prego are popular]

1 cup mozzarella cheese

Directions:

Place frozen stuffed shells in 13 x 9 inch rectangular baking dish. Cover shells with sauce.

Top with cheese, crushed red peppers or jalapenos to taste. Cover with aluminum foil and bake for 40 minutes at 425^0.

Enjoy!

Spicy Stuffed Shells Variations:
For decreased servings, halve recipe.
To feed a crowd, double recipe and add an extra 13 x 9 pan. Serves 8 people(16 stuffed shells).

MICROWAVE OVEN
#29 Loaded Baked Potatoes
Microwave time: 9 minutes   Microwave setting: High 4 servings

Ingredients:
4 medium baked potatoes
1 ½ cups Cheddar Cheese
¼ cup Bacon Bits
1 bunch broccoli florets, fresh or defrosted
½ cup low fat sour cream

Directions:
Slice top of potatoes from end to end, and place all 4 in microwave.

Bake until a fork goes into potatoes easily, about 10 minutes.
When done, squeeze ends together to 'crumble' potato in the skin.

Place florets, Bacon Bits and cheese over potatoes and microwave for 2 more minutes until cheese is melted and florets are warm and soft.

Serve with light sour cream.

Variations:
May top with beef chili, provolone or Swiss cheese, as well. A low calorie option would be to top with chunky salsa. Potatoes are naturally high in fiber and antioxidants and known well as being a healthy comfort food.

STOVETOP RECIPE
#30 Vegetable Beef Soup
Soup is the perfect healthy meal for chilly nights!
Cooking time: 40 minutes   Stove setting: Medium
8 Servings

Ingredients:
1 large box College Inn or Swanson's Beef Broth
1/3 cup beef bouillon granules
2 cups cut up, cooked beef chunks or shredded beef
1 package frozen mixed vegetables
1 cup barley, dry
½ box small seashell pasta or elbow pasta

Vegetable Beef Soup Directions:
Place all ingredients in a tall pasta pot, except pasta and barley, stirring occasionally for 30 minutes.

Bring to a boil and add pasta and barley to soup base, making sure to stir and separate pasta and barley to prevent clumping.

When pasta and barley are soft, plump, in about 10 minutes, stir again and turn stove temperature onto low.

Continue to cook on low until ready to eat, up to an hour.

To serve:
Serve in a bowl or mug with crackers or bread, or a grilled cheese sandwich. If soup is too hot to eat, place an ice cube in it to cool it down.

Especially good when you're not feeling well!

STOVETOP RECIPE

#31 Mommadele's
Chicken Noodle Soup

Cook for 30-60 minutes   Stove setting: Medium heat   Makes 8
                             servings

Mommadele's Chicken Noodle Soup Ingredients:
1-32oz box of College Inn or Swanson's Chicken broth
1/3 cup chicken bouillon granules
1 can chicken or 2 cups of cooked, cut-up chicken
10 Mini chopped carrots
1 stalk celery
½ box Linguine noodles, cooked or uncooked, broken
[add as desired]
1 cup water

Directions:
Place all ingredients in a tall pasta pot, stirring occasionally. Bring to a
soup base to a boil and add linguine to liquid making sure to stir and
separate pasta to prevent clumping. When linguine is cooked, in about 9
minutes, stir again and turn stove temperature onto low.

To serve:
Serve in a bowl or mug with crackers or bread, or a grilled cheese
sandwich. If soup is too hot to eat, place an ice cube in it to cool it a bit.

II. Kitchen Measures

3 teaspoons = 1 tablespoon

1 tablespoon = 3 teaspoons

¼ cup = 4 tablespoons

½ cup = 4 ounces

¾ cup = 6 ounces

1 cup = 8 ounces

2 cups = 16 ounces = 1 pint

3 cups = 24 ounces

4 cups = 32 ounces

1 pint = 16 ounces = 2 cups

2 pints = 64 ounces = 1 quart

4 pints = 1/2 gallon = 2 quarts

8 pints – 1 gallon – 4 quarts

1 liter = 128 ounces =1000ml

1 gallon = 8 pints = 4 quarts

III. Shortcut Cooking Terms

Bake: To cook with dry heat as in an oven.

Blacken: The result of coating fish or meat with Cajun seasoning and baking in oven or in skillet to give it a black color when heated.

Blend: To mix 2 or more ingredients fully.

Boil: To heat liquid until bubbles form on the surface

Broil: To cook under direct heat as in to broil in the oven.

Carmelize: To heat onions until they are brown

Chop: To cut food, such as in vegetables or fruit, into small pieces.

Dice: To chop into small pieces with a knife, chopper or other kitchen tool.

Drizzle: To lightly place a series of drops of liquid over food.

Flake: To separate into small pieces.

Garnish: To decorate food as with lemon wedges, slices, parsley, cilantro, oranges, and the like.

Mix: To combine ingredients as to stir.

Saute: To heat in pan or skillet or Wok until hot and brown in hot shortening.

Simmer: To cook slowly on low heat.

IV. Basic Kitchen Tools for Cooking

Wok pan
Frying pan
Stove splatter guard
Microwave cover
CrockPot Slow Cooker > 4-5 quarts
CrockPot Slow Cooker > 6-7 quarts for cooking for a crowd
Tall pasta pan with Lid
Spatula
2 cup measuring cup
Teaspoon measure
Tablespoon measure
Wooden spoons
Slotted spoon
Serving spoon
Mixing bowl
Paring knife
Kitchen cutting knife
Cutting board
Rectangular pan 13 x 9
Deep, round 9 inch pie pan
Manual Food Chopper
1 Serving plate
2 Serving bowls
Saran wrap
Aluminum foil
Ziplock bags

V. Dinner Pantry Grocery List

Pantry Foods
4 Uncle Ben's Ready Rice
Beef Bouillon
Chicken Bouillon
Chunky Salsa
Corn Taco Shells
Egg Noodles
Elbow Macaroni
Flour Tortillas
Linguine
Salt & pepper
Montreal Seasoning
Siracha Sauce
SoyVay Soy Sauce
Spaghetti
Spaghetti sauce
[Prego or Ragu are good]
Taco seasoning packet
Fajita seasoning packet
Campbell's Cream of Mushroom
Soup
Cream of Celery Soup
Canned Chicken [tuna aisle]
Olive oil
PAM Cooking Spray
Instant mashed potatoes
Canned corn
Canned black beans

Wondra Flour Mix
Potatoes

Freezer Foods
Frozen broccoli
Frozen Mixed Vegetables
Frozen Peas
Frozen Stuffed Shells
Frozen Thai Stir-Fry Vegetables
Texas Toast Garlic Bread
Chicken breasts
Beef chuck roast

Refrigerated foods
Shredded cheddar cheese
Lettuce,
Onions
 Green spring onions
Baby carrots
Chopped garlic
Pillsbury Roll-out Pie Crust

VI. SAMPLE WEEKLY DINNERS

Week I
Monday >>> Tijuana Tacos < Stovetop >
Tuesday>>> Busy Day Baked Chicken <Oven>
Wednesday >>> Chicken Cacciatore < CrockPot >
Thursday >>> Asian Rice Bowls < Stovetop >
Friday >>> Hearty Pot Roast < CrockPot >
Saturday >>> Tim's Tex Mex < Stovetop >
Sunday >>> Creamy Mac & Cheese < Stovetop >

Week II
Monday >>> Enrique Enchiladas <Oven>
Tuesday >>> Greek Omelet <Stovetop>
Wednesday >>> Cranberry Pork Chops <CrockPot>
Thursday >>> Saucy Mushroom Chicken <CrockPot>
Friday >>> Fiesta Fajitas < Stovetop >
Saturday>>>Almost Home-Style Spaghetti < CrockPot >
Sunday >>> Best Ever Maryland Crab Cakes < Oven>

Week III
Monday >>> Easy Thai Stir Fry < Wok/Stovetop >
Tuesday >>> Hawaiian Pineapple Chicken <CrockPot>
Wednesday >>> Beef Chili < CrockPot >
Thursday >>> White Chili < CrockPot >
Friday >>> Hot Sausage, Green Peppers & Onions < CrockPot >
Saturday >>> Fried Rice < Wok/Stovetop >
Sunday >>> Lo Mein < Wok/ Stovetop >

Week IV
Monday >>> Buffalo Chicken <Oven>
Tuesday >>> Cheddar Veggie Burgers < Stovetop >
Wednesday >>> Baked Fish Pockets <Oven>
Thursday >>> Spicy Stuffed Shells <Oven>
Friday >>> Pot Pie <Oven>
Saturday >>> Tuna Casserole <Oven>
Sunday >>> Kung Pao Chicken <Oven>

Week V
Loaded Baked Potato <Microwave>
Vegetable Beef Soup < Stovetop >
Chicken Noodle Soup < Stovetop >
Tijuana Tacos < Stovetop >
Chicken Cacciatore < CrockPot >
Hearty Pot Roast < CrockPot >
Asian Rice Bowls < Stovetop >

VII. LEFTOVER CITY

Leftovers in the fridge? Try these favorite recipes from *Mommadele's Easy Dinner Ideas for College Students...*

Chicken Leftover Ideas

#1 Tijuana Tacos < Stovetop >
#2 Chicken Cacciatore < CrockPot >
#3 Asian Rice Bowls < Stovetop >
#5 Tim's Tex Mex < Stovetop >
#8 Enrique Enchiladas <Oven>
#11 Saucy Mushroom Chicken <CrockPot>
#12 Fiesta Fajitas < Stovetop >
#15 Easy Thai Stir Fry < Wok/Stovetop >
#16 Hawaiian Pineapple Chicken <CrockPot>
#18 White Chili < CrockPot >
#21 Lo Mein < Wok/ Stovetop >
#26 Pot Pie <Oven>
#28 Kung Pao Chicken <Oven>
#31 Chicken Noodle Soup < Stovetop >

Beef Leftovers Ideas

#1 Tijuana Tacos < Stovetop >
#3 Asian Rice Bowls < Stovetop >
#4 Hearty Pot Roast < CrockPot >
#5 Tim's Tex Mex < Stovetop >
#8 Enrique Enchiladas <Oven>
#12 Fiesta Fajitas < Stovetop >
#15 Easy Thai Stir Fry < Wok/Stovetop >
#17 Beef Chili < CrockPot >
#21 Lo Mein < Wok/ Stovetop >
#26 Pot Pie <Oven>
#30 Vegetable Beef Soup < Stovetop >

Congratulations!

Now that you have completed this beginner's shortcut cooking guide, it is my express hope that you have adopted some new favorite recipes and learned how to make some old family favorites, as well. As you can see, cooking is an art, as each dish is unique even when made from a recipe. For like art, there is always more than one way to do things…even and especially while cooking…which is why many of the recipes in this book have variations for you to try.

Whether cooking for one, two or a crowd, I hope you find this cookbook easy to read and enjoy eating what you cooked for yourself and others. If you are new to cooking, perhaps this is just the beginning for you as you develop more and more culinary skills as you go along. As the old adage goes, "Practice makes perfect!"

Here's to many enjoyable years of cooking, for yourself and others!

Happy Cooking,
Mommadele

Made in the USA
Middletown, DE
10 December 2014